D0840814

Woman in the Painting

Woman in the Painting

For John —
with appreciation
to you for not allowing
the snow to keep you home.

Andrea Hollander Budy

5 December 2007
Pittsburgh

Autumn House
Press

PITTSBURGH

Autumn House Press Staff
Executive Director: Michael Simms
Community Outreach Director: Michael Wurster
Co-Director: Eva Simms
Technology Consultant: Matthew Hamman
Editorial Consultant: Ziggy Edwards
Media Consultant: Jan Beatty
Tech Crew Chief: Mike Milberger

In memory of Jack Wolford (1945-2005)

ISBN: 1932870113
Library of Congress Control Number: 2006922105

Also by Andrea Hollander Budy

The Other Life
Story Line Press, 2001

House Without a Dreamer
Story Line Press, 1993

What the Other Eye Sees (chapbook)
Wayland Press, 1991

Happily Ever After (chapbook)
Panhandler Press, 1989

Living on the Cusp (chapbook)
Moonsquilt Press, 1981

Acknowledgments

Grateful thanks to the editors of the journals in which the following poems were first published:

Arkansas Literary Forum: "Auden," "*Self-Portrait Between Clock and Bed*"

Arts & Letters: "Dead Weight," "Parts of Speech," "Still Life with Jonquils"

Big City Lit: "First Books"

Ellipsis: "The Life of Inanimate Objects"

FIELD: "Giving Birth"

Five Points: "East Third at Ocean," "For Weeks after the Funeral," "Weather"

The Georgia Review: "Abundance," "Beauty Parlor," "Ochre," "Spark," "Woman in the Painting"

The Hurricane Review: "Spaghetti"

Lake Effect: "Arrival"

Midwest Quarterly: "Remission"

Natural Bridge: "Wraith"

New Works Review: "First Love," "In the Garden"

Pleiades: "Larkin," "Sorrow"

Poetry: "Ellis Island, 1907," "Poem in October"

Prairie Schooner: "Nineteen-Thirty-Eight"

Rattapallax: "Dickinson"

Resurgence: "*Woman Holding a Letter*"

River City (The Pinch): "A Simple Story"

Runes: "In the Sixth Year of My Father's Illness," "Living Room"

Shenandoah: "Exchange Student," "Sunday Dinner"

Southern Poetry Review: "Emerson Fought His"

The Southern Review: "A Poem About Lust That's Not About Sex"

Sou'wester: "636 Lyons Avenue, Apartment 101," "Elegy for Gregory," "First Death," "Nineteen," "October 9, 1970," "Room 246," "Rue de Lyon"

"First Books" is also included in *What We Have: A Drift of White, a Wisp of Blue*, Martin Mitchell, ed. (Headwaters Press, 2004) and in *Never Before: Poems about First Experiences*, Laure-Anne Bosselaar, ed. (Four Way Books, 2005).

"Giving Birth" appears in *Writing Poems, 6th edition,* Robert Wallace & Michelle Boisseau, eds. (Addison, Wesley, Longman, 2003).

"The Life of Inanimate Objects" won the 2002 Ellipsis Poetry Award, selected by Philip Levine.

"Living Room" won the 2004 RUNES Award, selected by Jane Hirshfield, and was later collected, along with "In the Sixth Year of My Father's Illness," in the anthology, *Lasting: Poems on Aging,* Meg Files, ed. (Pima Press, 2005).

"Poem in October" appears in *The Autumn House Anthology of Contemporary American Poetry*, Sue Ellen Thompson, ed. Autumn House Press, 2005.

"Still Life with Jonquils" was featured on Poetry Daily (www.poems.com) on 10 September 2005.

Contents

III

IV

Still Life with Jonquils

The usual bowl of fruit, yes,
and at attention in a blue porcelain vase
wands of jonquils not yet bloomed,

gray-green buds
like translucent cocoons,
their wet and yellow wings

stirring against the thinning threads
of gray, about to give way –
the way a woman whose wrist

has been lightly touched beneath
the starched tablecloth recognizes
a man's invitation, its promise,

as the chatter of dinner guests blurs
into nonsense and she begins to feel
the invisible tug on the knot

fixed at the body's center
waiting
to be undone . . .

The painter knows
what not to execute, knows we bring
our own heat to the canvas,

knowing exactly how
these jonquils would look
if open.

But not letting them.

Abundance

It wasn't obvious, the way wealth glitters
from the finger or neck, the wrists.

I'm speaking of this other accumulation
inside the body,

invisible, yet we believed
we could feed on it,

though we could not see it,
could not prove it was there.

We were filled with envy, of course,
as if we were thin-haired women

and hers, thick, flowing to her waist,
her hips.

In her company we'd erase
ourselves, become her

mirror. When she smiled,
we'd smile back, when she lowered

her eyes or blushed, we'd do the same.
And when she showed us

the way a woman like her handles
serious disappointment, moving quickly

beyond it, acting as though it was the man
who had missed something,

shaking her head, pushing
her hair from her face,

her eyes nevertheless shining with forgiveness –
our eyes, too, would demonstrate

understanding, as if we too had succumbed
then been dismissed, knew

from experience what that was.
As if the man who had left her

had left us, and before that
had wanted us

the way
we had seen, had almost felt,

he had wanted her.

Dinner Party

And then, during dessert, she witnessed
a certain flicker in his eye. It felt to her

like frost that looks at first like dew
but by noon has turned everything brown.

The others went on with their faraway
laughter and complaints – the wrong man

at the helm, the sour job, rain at the beach,
crowds on the slopes.

Pay attention, her heart said now.
Follow his gaze, his torso.

Toward whom does he lean? Brush against
by accident?

One by one, she scrutinized the women,
remembered her once-upon-a-time self

across the damask cloth from him
and not much later

beneath him on the satin.

Johannes Vermeer, oil on canvas, 1663
Rijksmuseum, Amsterdam

The light is best by the open window in the front room.
A horse cobbles by and the brief shadow
of a bird she cannot name.
She unfolds the milk-white paper, its blue
words in their familiar script
and she knows
(before letting the voice of the words enter her
the way they entered her the night all this began)
that she will always know
the scrape of the postman's boot on the slate step
and his diminishing shape as he heads up the walk
and the scratch of the elderberry branch
against the house and the white petals
that descend in the slight breeze
like bits of translucent paper
and the distant mewing of a cat somewhere else
in the village, and when she folds the letter
back against itself, pressing its harsh white edges
together between her fingers, the way
the child inside her twists
as if he were a knot tightening.

Dickinson

I am older – tonight, Master – but love is the same –
"Master" Letter #3, 1861

So she gazed out the windows of her father's house,
first from the dining room, then the parlor, then
from her upstairs bedroom, south side first, then east.
Once even from the sliver of a window in the attic,
so narrow only the tops of the firs were visible.
But never did she see him coming, huddled
into himself, a tiny crow on the winter landscape
of Amherst. Never did she breathe in at the sight of him
wrapped in his black cape, tacking toward her into the wind.
Instead she faced the white paper of her longing,
her words exquisite as sweet cream, emphatic
as buttermilk. She imagined a bird here, a snake
on another page. She created a world
she began to believe in, believe it was enough,
a place a man like him wouldn't be afraid of, her own
shadow leaning over his.

Splashes of color on the cover,
lettering in wedding invitation script,
the name of the writer infinitesimally small
or so unreadably fancy it's clear
the designer is first-time too,
a novice at computer graphics
auditioning her wares.

But first-time authors keep
their disappointments
to themselves, preferring to believe
readers will pull them anyway
from bookstore shelves, will order
from Amazon, will forgive
their obviously first-time looks
the way first-time lovers forgive
the fumbling of belts, eyelets, straps,
happy enough to have finally
gotten this far, breathless
at the wonder of the other's
nakedness, sacred places
exposed, clumsy even in their
humbleness. And afterwards

the relief of having
the first time behind them
for the first time, filled
with forgiveness, and later,
alone, giggling at themselves
in a bathroom mirror, spotting
mascara on a nose, curious
if the other noticed a pair

of pimples on a chin –
then suddenly stricken,
afraid this first time
will be the only time
it will ever happen.

I have one scar. I scraped my foot against the reef.
You know how it is when something
so startles you into your life –
you forget you're anything but eyes
or ears or mouth. It doesn't have to hurt.
I'm talking about certain swells
of music your bones recognize
as if they created them and now
they've come home. Or the first drop
of honey on the tongue. The kiss
that overtakes the body, produces
secrets you didn't know it held.

Five feet down the world changes.
Close to the reef where the sun stretches in
you can sometimes see into constricted
caves and crevices. In and out of them rush
tiny translucent fish colorful as jewels. Deeper,
blue turns black, the underside rough
and unpredictable like a man's unexpected
hand on a first date.

Some fish accumulate
in the reef's pockets, then flash all at once
as if there's an odor pulling them.
Must be like the sweetness
of dawn when I lived above a bakery.
All that yeast rising through the floor boards.
My sleeping mouth watered,
waking me. This isn't supposed to be a poem
about sex, but if I were a woman allowed
to speak her hungers, it would be.

Nineteen

She didn't know what would happen
the first time she did it, hidden

at nearly midnight on the sudden slope
of the grassy hillside. Afraid

anyway of being caught, she kept
her eyes open, hardly mindful

of his breathy words
and his different kind of kissing

or this new, unremitting pressure
of his body. She felt the shadows

of lampposts hovering above them
like policemen with their hands

behind their backs. She remembered
from television the handcuffed hands

of the uni-bomber being led
into the courthouse in his orange uniform.

She imagined the secretary
who slit open

one of those letters and lost both hands.
Nor could she forget the missing legs

of a man she knew who'd fought
in World War II, nor the sound

of his wheelchair as he steered it
down the hall of his suburban house.

By then it was over.
Her own hands and legs had grown

numb, her lips sore, her intimate body
tender, swollen, spent. All of it

almost without her.

In the Garden

Mill Cottages, Donnington, England

A squirrel fidgets at the tip of a swaying branch
and I wonder if he clings without knowing he clings.

Sometimes I remember my first time
and wonder if that girl I was held any regrets.

I think about the boy I believed I would cling to forever,
whatever I understood *forever* to mean,

no more reliable than the wind that is blind to us
and invisible.

Of course we were both young and knew
only how much we didn't know,

both of us giddy with wanting.
The squirrel leaps. The branch holds.

That's where he is now, worrying another pine cone.
I've seen this before. And him. Or one just like him.

Later there were other men
and the hopes of a young woman,

a little older now, a little more equipped,
steadying herself and more sure of her place

in her own life, not counting on
even the sturdiest looking

branch to hold her.

First Love

Between two branches of juniper
the moon appears, white sliver
in the night sky. This is to say

I haven't forgotten you.
Forgotten how you turned
from the vestibule

and never
looked back, or the way
I stood on the stoop, listless

in the failing light, and watched
as you slumped down the street,
a dark figure blending

into the wreckage of late afternoon,
no one
to anyone else. This is to say

I no longer miss you, that in fact
I haven't thought of you in years.
But I remember still the sound

of early November leaves
and the smell of them
crushed beneath the tires of some car

that pulled to the curb just as you disappeared.
Tonight's moon
will not return tomorrow. Already it climbs

beyond the branches.
This is to say, no matter
how many others I've loved,

you remain
the first flicker in that night sky – singular,
before my eyes adjusted to the darkness.

Ex

Long after I married you, I found myself
in his city and heard him call my name.
Each of us amazed, we headed to the café
we used to haunt in our days together.
We sat by a window across the paneled room
from the table that had witnessed hours
of our clipped voices and sharp silences.
Instead of coffee, my old habit in those days,
I ordered hot chocolate, your drink,
dark and dense the way you take it,
without the swirl of frothy cream I like.
He told me of his troubled marriage, his two
difficult daughters, their spiteful mother, how
she'd tricked him and turned into someone
he didn't really know. I listened and listened,
glad all over again to be rid of him, and sipped
the thick, brown sweetness slowly as I could,
licking my lips, making it last.

I should name something so you'll know
just which yellow I mean, the ochre
of my bed shirt with the holes in one sleeve,

the ochre of the benches
at the corner of Boulevard Saint Louis, of the curtains
in the brushstrokes of Bonnard – his ochre palette,

the pallor of the woman's skin in the painting
I keep returning to. But it's not
just the color I like –

it's the sound, the way it hides in the tunnel
of the mouth without touching
anything: not the tongue that wants

to know if it tastes of syrup or salt,
not the teeth that could cut it in two
but only want to trace the shape of it,

not even the soft cheeks that seek to embrace
if only for the slightest moment
the deft word

as it enters, braces itself, hovers
like a swimmer at the edge
of a pool ready for the whistle, then escapes

into speech that dissipates before I can trap it.
So I say it sometimes – *ochre* –
just to savor the almost of it, the *O*

of my lips in the *O* of surprise
as the ochre passes through. And I spell it
the British way, *r* before *e,*

to give it that hint of unending.
So much like love it is, the way
I don't even know if it's two syllables

or one, the fickle way it simultaneously longs for
and turns away. There might be specks of ochre
in a lover's eyes, and on his neck

the faded color in the mark love left.
But always there's the delicious
pleasure that occurs as I say its name

the way I speak my lover's,
in almost a whisper, as if it were sacred –
say it, and say it, and say it again.

Her face has disappeared. This happens
more often than you think. She sits
at a table with her hands in her lap
beside her husband, his arms
folded over one another, blue bowls
and empty glasses set out before them
and a pitcher of translucent milk.

If the woman had eyes, they would be
the hazel eyes of my mother,
her sadness exposed. If a mouth,
my mother's, her upper lip
with the scar she hid with lipstick.
Like my mother, she would be better
at listening than speaking. Afternoons
after high school my friends would come
when their boyfriends tired of them.
They would sit at a table like this one,
white and gleaming with food,
and she would listen until it was time
for my father to return, her dark hair
pulled behind her ears, her silence
laconic and wise.

Perhaps the woman in the painting
tried to speak, as my mother did,
to her father, raising her face toward him
like the mutt she once begged for,
already cowering but finally unable

to utter a sound, language transformed
to movement, to the trembling body
suppliant before him, her pupils
suddenly large and black, tears
not yet formed but forming.

The husband's face is opulent, his eyes
the color of olives at the bottom of a drink.
Perhaps the woman believes the man
she married is only her husband. For a while
that's what we all think.

Always my grandparents arrived
disguised as harmless elders.
They'd say grace, bless the three
of us and our small residence
above my father's office.

Residence. I don't choose the word
for the poem's sake, but because
it was *their* word. I want you to hear
what I heard
through all those years

before my mother's death,
all those Sunday briskets
and pot roasts, all those potatoes
she and I peeled on Saturdays
and the pies whose crusts

we dispatched till it became ritual
the way, I thought, the making of the host
must be ritual for those who toil
in some secret bakery blessed
by a bishop. I haven't forgotten

I wrote *disguised.* And I know
you might wonder if I should have
changed that word
before I called this poem finished.
I meant

they had harmed someone.
Not me who believed
in the prayers they uttered,
but my mother
who inhabits me each time

I roll out the dough as she did,
shape it, fit it to the pan,
fill it with mincemeat or apples,
pinch the edges together
with my thumb and forefinger,

and with the tines of my fork
prick it and prick it and prick it.

We stood at the stove
waiting for the water to boil.
She held it in one hand,
always the right amount
for one meal. In the other
an ache shaping itself
as she told me of the afternoon
her father had come back from work
to their ground floor apartment
her last semester of high school,
and brought the snow with him,
his feet sounding at the vestibule
like a soldier's.
But this was New Jersey, 1938,
the Great War he never went to
over, the Great Depression
not yet named.
The desk job he held for years
over too, now he said
he would not take
the only job he could get,
shoveling coal with all those
black men – *would* not,
and she would have to quit school.
She swallowed hard,
tasting it again as we stood
together in that kitchen
with its sketches of happy
farmers and their mules pulling

wagons across the wallpaper.
The pot began to gurgle,
spitting its steam. I watched
as first the dry pasta stood
at attention in the water,
then fanned out, separating,
sinking, going limp.

I remember the way my mother
answered when people asked
where she'd gone to school:

South Side High, 1938,
adding the year in the same breath
though I knew

she never graduated,
yanked out
when her father lost his job.

Now it was her turn
to make herself
useful, he told her.

Hadn't he put
food on the table
all her life and all her little sister's?

How necessary
to tell a lie like hers, to answer
South Side High, 1938, and smile

without betraying
the blaze in her chest, her envy
for the questioner who likely met

her own husband at some university.
But wasn't my mother *the lucky one,*
my grandfather was fond of telling her

even into my childhood, sometimes
in front of my friends, lucky
to have got my father, a college man

who sat beside her at a ballgame
in 1939? *Just look at her
who didn't finish high school!*

Didn't I tell her then it wouldn't matter?

My Grandmother Taking Off My Grandfather's Shoes

Every day after work he'd sit in his armchair
with its antimacassar and its plush burgundy velour
and she'd kneel on the floor to unfasten the laces,
loosen the tongues, and lift out his feet.
When I was ten I stayed for a week
and did it for her. He thought I did it
for him.

Beauty Parlor

One of the regulars had cancer
in those days before chemo,
and even after the beautician lowered
the hairdryer canister over the woman's head,

she talked nonstop about the intense heat
of cobalt treatments, the way her body burned
in places she'd rather not name,
how her skin there felt more like leather.

When she paused, the beauty parlor grew
strangely quiet: only the hum of the dryers,
the occasional whoosh of water at the sinks.
Until she spoke again, no one looked at her.

Then she droned on, but this time
about her son, who'd stopped coming by
now his wife had him
wound around her little finger.

I didn't understand yet
it wasn't his wife that kept the son away.
I was seventeen and only a guest
in this world

where my mother was a regular
on Wednesdays. That day she sat up front
among the women's magazines.
After I was done, we'd go to lunch.

And in a few days she'd tell me
her own bad news. She'd say she didn't want
to spoil my senior prom. But that afternoon
as the woman carried on and on and on,

she already knew what she knew.

Dandelions

After learning the cancer had spread

When I was ten I earned
a nickel for each dandelion
I dug out of the front lawn.
For the first time I looked closely
and saw how lovely they were,
imagined letting them grow,
a yellow rug rolled out on the lawn,
our yard the only yellow one in town.
Cars would slow, especially on Sundays,
and grandmothers in white gloves
would point from rolled-down windows,
*oo*ing and *ahh*ing.

Those yellow flowers faded, then vanished,
replaced by hairy, gray surrogates
that invaded the neighborhood, especially
the yards of abandoned houses or the ones
whose owners didn't seem to mind.

When our own grass
grew perfect and green
and my parents forbade me
to even walk on it, we kids
invaded those yards, too. In those days
before any of us understood
our bodies could betray us, we blew
dandelion spores into each others' faces
and into the late spring air, not knowing
where they'd take hold, not caring.

They chewed with their mouths open,
my grandparents. I knew better
than to mention it, though my mother
who'd grown up in that apartment
who'd sat between them
where I sat now
would have given me
one of her looks.
She was in the hospital
again. Stripped
of hope this time
that she'd ever leave,
I'd come to eat with them,
these two who that evening
knew themselves
only as her parents
but seemed more like children
learning for the first time
appropriate behavior
as they sat
at the oilclothed table,
paper napkins on their laps
and cut their meat
without any help from me.

Spark

Because each small spark must turn to darkness
in its own way, the garden snake blooms

larger from each of its skins until the one
it dies in. Upside down in the underbrush,

the turtle stills, all its tiny bones collapsed
inside its shell. The stalks of lavender

clipped from the garden for the dresser
never let go their relentless odor

that dominates still the chest
that belonged to my mother.

And my mother herself, in and out
of the hospital those last weeks,

in between
bought six new dresses, a sewing machine,

and when she couldn't sleep, studied books
of wallpaper samples.

I hung the shopping bag
on the knob inside
the wide door of the bathroom,
draped my sweater and jeans,
even my bra, over the metal bar,
careful not to disturb
the white hospital towel
that hung there.

The dress was red and sleek,
rare for me at twenty-three,
but I wanted to be
someone else, do something
someone else might do.
Low-cut back
nearly to my waist,
scalloped neckline
almost to my breasts.
I pinched my cheeks,
bit my lips, stepped out
without my shoes
just as the night nurse
hustled in
with her packet of pills
and scowled.

But I watched
the approving eyes
of my mother instead,
her bed cranked up

so she wouldn't need
to lift her head, and how she
signaled with her hand for me
to spin and spin as if
it were already Saturday night
and some young man she'd never
get the chance to meet
had asked me to dance.

The same automatic doors
and the same white-haired volunteer,
the elevator and the corridor
with its antiseptic odor
and hushed voices
door after door
down one more hall and again
through the double doors –
but this morning
the lone nurse standing
before the door of 246,
and immediately inside,
the view through the window
of the other wing,
its dozens of identical windows,
and here the pale green walls
paler today behind the blank
screen of the TV
protruding from the wall
and on the movable
metal bedside table
the familiar plastic glass of water
with its bent straw
peering out like a periscope
through its plastic lid
as if only a hidden eye
had full view of the bed
and the body of the woman in it
who was once my mother.

Wedding Band

My father went in first,
had me wait outside the door.

I can't remember what I thought
in those trying minutes trying

not to think at all.
A child and her mother

wandered down the hall.
I may have wondered

how one so young had been allowed
to break the rules.

This is the worst day of my life,
my father said and called me in.

It's hard now to know
if I noticed right away

the missing ring she'd refused ever
to remove even when she swam

or bathed. I know I saw the lack
of pain or struggle in her face.

I wondered what they'd do
with all those flowers.

Her hair flailed reckless from her head,
her hands lay folded on her chest.

Did he have to work
to pull it

from her finger
or did it loosen on its own?

Weather

This is a poem with no heavenly planets
to keep track of, no rain pelting the abandoned
parking lot. It is cold, November, evening,
but you will barely detect the scrawny
woman wrapped in only a borrowed raincoat
making her way up Cranford Avenue after
her sister's funeral, because the streetlamps
are not on, those imitation moons.

And the snow, a few days old and already
dozed from the streets, scraped or blown
from the sidewalks, is barely worth mentioning,
because in her grief she doesn't see it,
and without the light of the moon or
the headlights of some driver on late shift,
even her puffs of breath are not visible.

This is how she will remember this night:
this weatherless air, this rude darkness,
this Cranford Avenue where the two of them
walked the length of their childhoods.
And she will remember this silence
disturbed by the sound
of only herself still breathing.

The house felt like the opera,
the audience in their seats, hushed, ready,
but the cast not yet arrived.

And if I said anything
to try to appease the anxious air, my words
would hang alone like the single chandelier

waiting to dim the auditorium, but still
too huge, too prominent, too bright, its light
announcing only itself, bringing more

emptiness into the emptiness.

Sorrow

Sometimes it's so large
we begin to be pulled under,

so large we believe we will drown
unless the plug is pulled

and it begins to drain away
through unseen pipes that usher it

out of the sad house
and below the neglected lawn

beneath the wide street and traffic,
beyond the traffic light

and the elementary school on the other side.
Underground it slowly, steadily dissipates

into the neighborhood beyond the playground
with its innocents at recess.

For so many years I was one of them.
From the top of the slide

I could spot our beige split-level
and even its flagstone walkway.

I could sometimes make out the silhouette
of my mother retrieving letters

from our mailbox
or out on the front lawn positioning

the oscillating sprinkler.
How good her timing was then,

not leaving it in one place too long
or letting the water wet the sidewalk,

never allowing it to drown
the things she planted.

Poem in October

After Dylan Thomas

It was my twenty-third year and heaven
broke away from my reach as I stood

at her grave. Rain carved
the morning's stone face into the earth,

and the sky grayed and lowered
until they were one. Back by the trees

men smoked, as if they had nothing
better to do. But I knew as soon as I left

they would cover even
the roses my father, brother and I

had tossed upon her as if our wishing
could do what prayer had not.

When I finally left, I thought her
gone. I am fifty-four. I was wrong.

Fist

Years later I drove by the house
where my father
bore his childhood.

It had been green then, or gray,
he couldn't remember –
like a series

of fading bruises
it was difficult to tell which
was the deepest layer.

Not a single tree, and only a few
stray weeds in the hard pack.
Torn screens, shades

instead of curtains,
round-topped front door
without a window.

I wished
I had seen that house before.
How much it might have explained.

I should have stopped the car
that afternoon and struck
the door with my fist,

struck one thing
acceptable to strike.

While the family slept, he scraped out innards.
Fox, badger, rabbit, mink – the rich
would have their jackets and stoles,
their long coats. The uniform he wore
belonged to the factory, but the boots
were his own. Blood on their soles, the perpetual
stench of blood in his nostrils. He did it
for his mother, good woman his father
had left, and his four siblings. During his break
in the factory courtyard, he'd nibble yesterday's
dark bread, gulp watered-down milk
from the thermos he'd used at school,
the air ruined by cigarettes and the blood
they'd all dragged with them. Light blared
from the building's windows.
If there were stars, he couldn't find them.
He'd shuffle back through the steel doors
and hold his breath like the brown boy
who would amaze him decades later
holding his breath for tourists who threw
coins into deep water for him to retrieve.
They'd shine from his palms
or his teeth when he surfaced, rising
from his poverty.

He wore it when he mowed the grass, walked the dog,
lounged with the Sunday papers. Whether
it was his favorite, I'm not sure, the way
I'm not sure if he cared for me
more than for my brother. When I was a child,
he would pull me aside sometimes
and tell me a secret – perhaps about his sister
or one of the brothers he wasn't speaking to,
a few times about my mother, whom I knew he loved –
but always something that nagged at him.

Afterwards he would tell me not to tell anyone,
then walk away whistling the way
Alec Guinness, in *The Bridge on the River Kwai,*
walked away whistling when they let him out
of solitary confinement, as if he knew
something wonderful and important
and no one could scare it out of him.
Sometimes at dinner, my father would whistle
that same tune. And wink at me.

How I loved being in cahoots with him. Loved
feeling chosen, being the one selected to receive.
I took each secret into me and kept it.

A Simple Story

Through the kitchen window the first
red streaks of October in the sweetgum leaves,
low clouds, the monotonous street bleak
and empty of traffic, except for an occasional
truck, its grumble of gears I've grown so
used to all my years in that house I barely hear it.
At the Formica table, I envision the grandfather
I've never met: ghostlike, skeletal, his cheeks gaunt,
his blue eyes shallow with loneliness.
Why did you leave? I ask, the story my father told
all my life: his father leaving his wife and five kids
and never looking back. *Oh, that*, he says,
as if I'd handed him a penny he'd dropped
and has to stop to examine, only to find
something common and nearly worthless.

The hands of the electric clock hesitate,
then tock soundlessly. *Complicated story,*
he says, raising his coffee cup
to his mouth, sipping, putting it down.
Rain has begun, pelting, curtaining
the window glass. The room darkens,
though it is early morning. I know
he won't say anything more, though
I will wait through the storm, wait
for the sky to change, the way in real life
I sit with my ailing father at this same
table of my childhood, smiling at him,
waiting for him to speak, touching his hand
or his arm, wanting to touch his face
but not wanting to frighten or distract him
as he trembles to remember who I am.

I tried to be careful. It lounged along the left side
of the bowl, the smallest I've ever seen, a dot
with legs. An asterisk. I turned the water
only slightly on and aimed the thin stream
directly toward the drain and watched the spider
squat on all eight miniscule legs and raise itself again.
But after I brushed my teeth the full two minutes
to appease my dentist and held the foamy brush
under the water and flicked the bristles
with my thumb to help release the minty suds,
I forgot it was there, and opened the faucet
full force and rinsed my mouth and spat,
and saw too late the dark speck spiraling down.
And I began to understand how it happened
that after the doctor announced the bleak diagnosis
and looked down at his silent desk, my father said,
as if it were someone else whose life and death
they were discussing, *Oh, isn't that sad.*

Glass of Water

When I handed him the glass
he stared as if it were something
he'd never seen.

He took it in both hands,
a wriggling fish he had to calm,
and steadied it.

Through the glass I could see
his concave face, distorted
as a trout being pulled

to the surface by its lip.
And when he drew it
to his own lips and drank,

he seemed not to notice
the tiny trail of water
wandering down his stubbled chin,

and I remembered the afternoon
they made him Lieutenant,
those extra stripes shining

from beneath his epaulettes.
He was forty. I was ten.
The night before, my mother

stayed up late to sew them on.
I sat in the bleachers that intense
Texas afternoon

and through field glasses watched
a pair of green iridescent flies
promenade along the lines

of sweat on my father's smooth
cheek and neck. He stood
at full attention in his wool uniform.

In the Sixth Year of My Father's Illness

I wonder if he remembers the jay
that flew into the living room window

that first day he introduced himself
to the neighbor he'd known forty years.

It lay among the crushed
pine bark we spread the previous May

around the roses where the roots were smooth
and thornless, that jay so blue and *too beautiful*

to move, he said. And it stayed beautiful
even as the ants paraded in and out of its head,

removing little bits to their underground country.
Afterwards its body lay still

and still beautiful, as if death had not yet
occurred to it, its feathers

blue as the sky it once knew so well,
that sky it mistook

for the real thing. Some truths
we cannot learn. Some we forget,

as my father did, who yesterday
introduced himself to me.

by labeling everything in his house –
its name, its use. Clock:
the thing that counts time.
Umbrella: the thing that strangers take away.

Sundays I phone my father's house
to hear his voice. *It's Andrea,* I say,
your daughter. Telephone: the thing
that says it is your daughter.

Living Room

In the cave of memory my father
crawls now, his small carbide light
fixed to his forehead, his kneepads
so worn from the journey they're barely
useful, but he adjusts them
again and again. Sometimes
he arches up, stands, reaches, measures
himself against the wayward height
of the ceiling, which in this part of the cave
is at best uneven. He often hits his head.
Other times he suddenly
stoops, winces, calls out a name,
sometimes the pet name he had
for my long-dead mother
or the name he called his own.

That's when my stepmother tries
to call him back. *Honeyman*, she says,
one hand on his cheek, the other
his shoulder, settling him
into the one chair he sometimes stays in.

There are days she discovers him
curled beneath the baby grand,
and she's learned to lie down with him.
I am here, she says, her body caved
against this man who every day
deserts her. *Bats,* he says, or maybe,
field glasses. Perhaps he's back
in France, 1944, she doesn't know.
But soon he's up again on his knees,

shushing her, checking his headlamp,
adjusting his kneepads, and she rises
to her own knees, she doesn't know
what else to do, the two of them
explorers, one whose thinning
pin of light leads them, making
their slow way through this room
named for the living.

My Father's Brain

Not a house
empty of its furniture

but an abandoned landscape
once punctuated
by sunlight, freshened by rain.

Once fluttering
with bobwhites and titmice,
the wispy calls all night
of whippoorwills,
jays bluing the shadows,
hawks mimicking the willful breeze,

and sometimes monarchs,
nearly identical pieces of stained glass,
settling momentarily
on branches of mulberry,
stalks of rye grass, fields.

Springs came, left, winters piled on.
Oak trees were harvested for lumber,
pine trees for pulp, burgeoning sassafras
removed for its root, cedar and juniper
cut for their spines, longstanding hickories
toppled by storms.

The rest – mown down
by wind, withered by sun.

Now only the shape of a place:
slight rises where children may have played,
houses may have stood,
pock marks in hollows
that signify graves.

Look, how tiny down there,
look: the last village of words and, higher,
(but how tiny) still one last
farmhouse of feeling.
  – Rainer Maria Rilke,
  "Exposed on the cliffs of the heart"

1

That first cruel day when my father
gazed into the bathroom mirror,
steam condensed enough to make him believe

it a window, did he fear
the proximity of that other face
glaring wildly at him through the glass?

Did he wonder if it came to taunt him,
or – worse – to take him, part by part,
first memory, then language, then the body itself?

Where does the consummate self exist?
Or are there parts, like parts of speech,
each with a separate purpose,

a single aspect of the whole
magnificence? Are there separate births,
separate passings?

He no longer fits
meanings to words, mere sounds
similar as the cars he watches

from his chair at the living room window,
no longer Oldsmobile or Dodge, names

he taught my brother and me, now
only a hum passing through the scenery.

2

Though hair whitens and skin lets go,
wisdom is supposed to accumulate, gather
kindling, add to the small fires that make up a life.

But some minds smolder. My once-wise father
now reaches for only a few certainties (that once
he studied French and fought in World War II)

and holds them
like lit candles he is afraid to walk with.
Like him, they diminish as they burn.

When you greet him
he salutes you. *Parlez-vous français?
Parlez-vous? Vous?*

3

Which word was first
to fade away? Which spark
failed again and again
to ignite?
As if the stars, one by one,
shut down.
Night comes and comes,
gently at first, but all day long
and stays.

4

He's like the very words
he no longer remembers,
the words themselves
elders we shun
with whole histories on their tongues,
but no one asks them anymore
what they know. They shuffle
to the well in bedroom slippers.
They drink from a tarnished cup,
remnants of insects' wings
floating on the surface.

5

Today my father will not bother
to look in the mirror for that other man
who has grown so stooped and silent.
Neither speaks. Twins, they lean
into their aluminum walkers, inch
across the bathroom toward the toilet.
When the mirror ends, one of them
disappears, as always,
into the invisible world.

Dead Weight

When he fell out of bed
and she couldn't lift him,
it took two men to put him back.
Then he slept, but not she,
who tried to count his breaths,
which sometimes slowed,
sometimes speeded up.
When he's least himself
she holds his hands,
stares into his face,
reminds him of her name.
These days he's so remote
she isn't sure he's really there.
She remembers
watching snow pile up
when she was a child,
the clear white shape
of her bicycle left
on the edge of the driveway,
and later only a trivial bump
within the blank white landscape.

All night he came to me, speaking
in the old way, shaping particular words,
meant words, phrases filled with purpose,
trenchant sentences sliding from his tongue,
an avalanche of language, a huge accumulation
of meaning upon meaning, coming fast,
faster, all at once, as if the side of the mountain
couldn't hold anymore, heavy and wet –
he who had been expert,
famous for leading others,
me, for example, to the top
or leaving us behind,
from where he viewed everything
beneath him: valleys, villages, invisible people
who couldn't imagine anyone,
even him, reaching such a place
or skiing down alone, taking charge,
making his magnificent mark
until all of it – words, phrases, sentences –
became one thing, solid and white,
breaking away *en masse*, and taking him
no matter who he was, with it.

IV

She misses
the slowness of things, the small
room built only for tea. Pungent
steam. The certainty of it. Here

there are too many closets,
the bed is soft and high. Not
the sweet mat made of rice chaff
rolled out each night, rolled back

when the light returns. At home
doors slide away, walls disappear
into other walls, and the landscape
enters: bird, cloud, tree, mist

sifting the daylight. Here
everything seems to happen
at once. Except in the Eastern wing
of the city museum the day

her host family took her,
where the white-gloved curator
unrolled the ancient scroll –
in order to see one scene

he had to roll away another.
And later how she stood
before the Western still life:
a palpable bowl of fruit, a slim

paring knife on the oil cloth like
the one her mother's mother used,
a single lemon, its thin peel curling
off the table and beyond the frame,

tenuous as the sloughed skin
of a garden snake. She could almost
smell the tartness of that yellow,
almost hear summer wasps

shifting into that room,
into that air she could breathe.

When her father stopped speaking
it was always to punish. Perhaps she left
the sprinkler sputtering

and flooded the lawn or used a kitchen fork
in the garden. Then, for a day or more
he'd walk past her in the hallway,

or go on eating his toast at breakfast,
dipping it again and again into his coffee,
as though she were only a window

he wasn't in the mood to look through.
Most days she did her chores
with her mouth closed, her mind

to herself, and sometimes for weeks
nothing went wrong.
On the way to school he might suggest

they sing together in the car, impressed
at the long stretch of her good behavior.
The most she ever spent on gifts

she spent on his – an Egyptian leather
wallet he wouldn't use until his old one
fell apart, the painting he'd hung

in their darkest hall so it wouldn't be "ruined"
by light. One night she heard
her mother's cracked voice, ghostlike,

pleading, she suspected, to her father's back,
then to the fleurs-de-lis thriving
on the wallpaper. If they could have,

they would have answered.

Edvard Munch by Himself: An Exhibition of 150
Self-Portraits, Royal Academy, London, 2005

He risked himself as the naked
Christ spiked to the cross,
scorned by the crazy mob.
Portrayed his own body
as the dead Marat in the famed tub,
his own head on Salomé's tray.
And again and again as a feckless man
whose vacuous eyes stare out from a face
imposed upon a darkness.

Then he's a middle-aged man seated alone
in a restaurant, three other figures
merely elements of composition
and mute as wallpaper.

Forty years later he's this dark silhouette
standing between a black grandfather clock
and his single bed – arms limp at his sides,
his face solemn, tired,
the only light a sharp yellow shaft
flourishing in another room
behind him.

Elegy for Gregory, Drowned at Twenty-three

> *The ocean is so beautiful, when I first saw it I cried like a baby.*
> – Gregory James

I can nearly feel that first joy
when it was no longer a calendar photograph

in his childhood room
or a bad painting in some motel, an image

he must have dismissed until finally
he walked onto his first beach and saw

how accurate the painter had tried to be,
how impossible its subject.

And then to enter that water, timid at first,
then playful, the glee in his face that spread

through his whole body. Perhaps he behaved
like an infant, the way my own son

discovered his toes,
amazed they were part of him.

And then, inevitably, I imagine those last minutes
when the sea showed

its hard beauty, the sun brilliant,
as the tide rose and rose, and he

a jewel sparkling, floating, pulled
farther and farther out.

And now I feel his fear,
nearly impossible not to imagine.

Not that the ocean wanted him.
Not that it wanted anything at all.

The moon shone that night
over the calm slosh of the sea,

its diminishing line of foam
thin and delicate and ribbony.

First Death

> *After the first death there is no other.*
> – Dylan Thomas

Mine was Jimmy Romeo in eighth grade,
whose identical twin stayed home the night
Jimmy rode our downtown streets
in the passenger seat with Frank Briggs,
also thirteen, at the wheel of his mother's car.
The two of them so bored, Frank had grabbed
her keys and two six packs
from the stack by the back door
of his dull and empty house.
They'd finished two
by the time Frank reached
for another and didn't see the tree.

In school that day we'd learned
the term *deus ex machina*. I thought
it was a cheesy way to end a play
and raised my hand.
Life doesn't happen that way, I said,
wanting from the text some kind
of common sense.

No gods appeared that night
to lift Jimmy from the car
in time. Nor all those endless days
the rest of junior high and high school
as the bell shot us from our seats
into the crowded halls between classes,
sometimes passing Jimmy's twin
or – worse – stumbling into Frank –
wishing for those gods to save us.

After it was published, he cursed
his poem, "September 1, 1939,"
its "incurable dishonesty," as if the worst
infection had taken hold of him
that awful day in some bar
on 52nd Street, New York City,
jotting it out
an ocean away from home,
the world again at war
and all his lines corrupt,
stubbing out a cigarette
in the full ashtray,
trying to match his private voice
to a public good.

Writing of helplessness
he felt helpless himself.
When he wrote
I and the public know
What all schoolchildren learn,
Those to whom evil is done
Do Evil in return,
on the page even truth
felt fraudulent. He could believe
only in his own failure.

And yet tonight, the 11th of September 2001,
as I drove home late with my son
on a gravel road halfway across the nation,
a radio commentator read the poem
at the close of a call-in show
meant to help us cope, and I

imagined Auden 62 years before,
picturing the Blitz in his own country,
hunched over his words,
dismissing his puny efforts,
never imagining
my son and me leaning into one
another, hearing in the voice
of the commentator
the poet's voice,
and needing it.

Rather than words comes the thought of high windows. . .

Always he preferred to look down on things:
the rooftops of shorter houses, the row
of treetops haloed by insects and birds,

automobiles stopped at the traffic signal on the corner,
men in hats on their way home from offices,
bare-headed women whose faces

he presumed beautiful,
pushing their carriages, walking their hounds.
The air at the top

had always been worth climbing to.
From here he could view
flowers in solid groups instead of rose by rose,

and girls – that other kind of bouquet – in uniforms,
their knee-socked legs gliding
beneath them.

When only the lamplights shone,
he'd make his predictable way to the pub
and stay until the other regulars

dropped away to girlfriends or wives.
He wasn't lonely. He'd even stopped writing.
Nothing else to say, he told anyone who asked,

nothing respectable that didn't sound arrogant
or foolish or, anyway, nothing worth trying
to fit a rhyme around – nothing, after he had written it,

that didn't bloody look down on him.

Ellis Island, 1907

Unless the officials could pronounce and spell a
name, every Eastern European Jew on the ship from
Rotterdam became a Hollander.

Sadie, who was only eight, wrote each letter down:
Haych, she said as she wrote it,
Oh, Ell. She had two countries now:
the one rising ahead of her like leavened bread
and the one her father said had saved them
that now would name them.
Out with the bad, in with the good,
her mother said. *Khollander*
she practiced saying, over and over,
new food in her mouth,
and dropped the name she was born with
like a baby's gummed zwieback.
She wrote it down again and again
trying it out, a bride-to-be, wondering
who she would become with a name like this
in this place
where she could become it.

East Third at Ocean

Six o'clock. A few teenagers take a final swim,
shake out towels, brush sand from their bodies.
So many lost sounds, thinner than money, thinner
than a trivial thought. Behind a young boy going home

the ocean hushes. The streets, too, begin to empty,
and a few men wander into the local tavern
where it is always the same: dark mornings
become dark afternoons, and only a human voice

answers the small prayer of the woman unable
to rise from the bar. Outside
the municipal clock strikes its whole note, unnoticed,
as though an afterthought.

In separate apartments a block from the beach,
a cradle rocks, a woman's head lolls over the day's news,
a sleepy man touches his lover's cheek
with his own cheek. And in every room

sunlight narrows, retreats. In an old house closer in,
a girl's fingers rise from the keys, and yet the melody lingers.
Predictably, darkness comes
but nothing important ends because of it, nothing stops,

nothing closes. Even the wordless voice of a newborn
blends into the waning day and goes on,
mocking the way you insist
on your own significance or try to separate

mornings from afternoons, days from other days, plain years
from the years of beautiful complication –
the way you behave
as if the ocean itself were not repetitive, endless.

Rue de Lyon

Above the tall buildings, above the tabac on the corner
and the small café,
the épicerie with its outdoor
fruitstand and its burgundy awning,
and across the street, too, over the boulangerie
and the laverie and the shop that sells paper and pens,
over all the wooden double doors that mark
entrances to courtyards and apartments,
over people in their small cars and the ones
hurrying by foot on the sidewalks – above all these,
clouds thicken, they shift and spit, they darken,
and rain begins in large droplets (they could almost be counted
then it falls in ribbons, in sheets.
Traffic dawdles, headlights flicker,
apartment shutters slam shut. And beyond the clouds,
something growls, then hurls down
its few inscrutable syllables, growls again, speaks again,
as though repetition were translation, a question the woman
huddled in one doorway could answer, as though
she might raise her face toward that unintelligible voice
and acknowledge her small place
under the canopy of one doorway where nearby
in the concrete sidewalk
the tiniest green clover has taken root
in a hole no larger than a centime
and is drenched in the downpour
and for a while longer, therefore, lives on.

Giving Birth

In time you won't even remember the pain.
– All the books on childbirth

On your back, heels locked in metal stirrups,
this immense volcanic shuddering
goes on against your will
as if it *were,* in fact, a volcano,
and your previous life merely a village of innocents
living on the island, used to it, barely mindful,
going about their daily repetitions, looking up
at each agitation only for a moment, thinking
it's nothing really, then returning
to their business, yanking the cord
of a lawnmower, mopping a kitchen floor,
licking stamps and sticking them one by one
onto a stack of sealed invitations.
And then again the mountain shudders.
Shudders again, this time violently.
But you are inside your breathing now, as you were taught,
and your husband's voice, his breath, that practiced duet now real,
the holding back, the pushing, the pain holding you
in its deep claws until there is nothing else.
And then the mountain erupts – you are sure of it –
erupts and erupts, its molten liquid
pushing beyond you, out, out
of your power, out, out. You wonder
where it will empty, what it will do
to those villagers who thought they had time.
Now there's no looking back, it's coming,
coming, and one of them
cries out – you hear him clearly, surely
as you heard your own pure cry moments ago,
or is this your own voice, or some part of your life

so distant it's barely attached even to memory, the way
volcanic ash showers cities hundreds of miles away,
where later the wind might shift
and a young man rising
onto the street from the metro,
brushes a bit of soot from his face.

for Marine Viennet

In Arkansas it is late afternoon
when our plane touches down
though I have left
part of myself in France
where hours ago the sun felt its way
down the wall of the ancient church
at St. Thiébaud and will climb
the other side while I am finally
in my own bed dreaming myself
still wholly there, where yesterday
we leaned against that same wall
after our day-long walk,
replenishing ourselves,
passing the canister of water
from one to the other to the other
as the sky began to dim
and my son, who lives in your country,
pointed to the white line being left
by a jet we couldn't see,
which reminded me of Hansel
who thought it would be easy
to follow the marked path back.

Remission

The grass hums with its bees and its mowers,
a breeze rises,

and leaves you would not have seen yesterday
lift and settle, lift and wander

a few at a time, yard to yard. Today
you wander, too, away from the house,

the neighborhood, along the road and up
through the pin oaks and pines that cover the hill.

In the hollow on the other side you stop
among the apple trees now empty

except for a few small fruits too high for anyone's reach.
You have never been this rich.

You lie on the rare ground, that small truth you had
somehow not counted on, sweet

with the wine of fallen apples,
empty and sweet yourself, nearly drunk

on the sound of your own breath
rising in its bounty from your mouth.

"Dandelions" was written for Roger Beal.

"In the Garden" is for Judith Burnley.

"Living Room" and "Dead Weight" are dedicated to Evelyn Zucker Hollander.

"Remission" was written for Kathleen Lynch.

Line 1 of "Spark" comes from Philip Levine's "My Son and I."

The following people devoted time and offered valuable feedback on individual poems and, in a few cases, the entire manuscript, which benefited from their attention: Peter Abbs, Sandra Slaughter Barnett, Suzanne Evans Blair, Sally Browder, Brooke Sparrow Budy, Judith Burnley, Deborah Cummins, Lisa Dart, Elizabeth Lacey Harris, David Jauss, Laurie Kutchins, Kathleen Lynch, Sandy Michel, Terrell Tebbetts, Virginia Wray, and especially Todd Budy, my first reader.

Appreciation to Carol Houck Smith for believing in and promoting the collection.

I am very grateful to St. Bede's School for a fruitful writing residency, and to Lyon College, where I could not ask for more supportive colleagues.

Thanks for honors and attentions from Lycée Montchapet and Université de Bourgogne, especially Anne-Marie Valour, Geneviève Duss, Fabienne Drag, Jacques Fuselier, and Sylvie Crinquand.

Michael Simms is a superlative editor. I am indebted to him and to the Autumn House Press staff for their work in bringing this book forth so wonderfully well.

The Autumn House Poetry Series

Michael Simms, Editor

OneOnOne
Jack Myers

*Snow White Horses,
Selected Poems 1973-1988*
Ed Ochester

*The Leaving,
New and Selected Poems*
Sue Ellen Thompson

Dirt
Jo McDougall

Fire in the Orchard
Gary Margolis

*Just Once,
New and Previous Poems*
Samuel Hazo

The White Calf Kicks
Deborah Slicer
2003 Autumn House Poetry Prize,
selected by Naomi Shihab Nye

The Divine Salt
Peter Blair

The Dark Takes Aim
Julie Suk

Satisfied with Havoc
Jo McDougall

Half Lives
Richard Jackson

Not God After All
Gerald Stern
with drawings by Sheba Sharrow

Dear Good Naked Morning
Ruth L. Schwartz
2004 Autumn House Poetry Prize,
selected by Alicia Ostriker

A Flight to Elsewhere
Samuel Hazo

Collected Poems
Patricia Dobler

*The Autumn House
Anthology of Contemporary
American Poetry*
edited by Sue Ellen Thompson

Déja Vu Diner
Leonard Gontarek

Lucky Wreck
Ada Limón
2005 Autumn House Poetry Prize,
selected by Jean Valentine

The Golden Hour
Sue Ellen Thompson

Woman in the Painting
Andrea Hollander Budy

Text and cover design by Kathy Boykowycz
Cover painting by Brooke Budy

Text set in Stone Serif, designed in 1987 by Sumner Stone
Titles set in Univers 67, designed in 1957 by Adrian Frutiger

Printed by Thomson-Shore of Dexter, Michigan,
on Natures Natural, a 50% recycled paper